Giggles, Gags and Groaners

BRAIN TEASERS

WRITTEN BY:

STUART A. KALLEN

Published by Abdo & Daughters, 6535 Cecelia Circle, Edina, Minnesota 55439.

Library bound edition distributed by Rockbottom Books, Pentagon Tower, P.O. Box 36036, Minneapolis, Minnesota 55435.

Cover Illustration: Terry Boles
Inside Illustrations: Terry Boles

Edited by: Rosemary Wallner

LIBRARY OF CONGRESS CATALOGING-IN-PUBLICATION DATA

Kallen, Stuart A., 1955-
        Brain Teasers/written by Stuart A. Kallen
                p. cm.--(Giggles, Gags and Groaners)
        Summary: A collection of brain teasers ranging from the easy to the bewildering.
        ISBN 1-56239-130-5
        1. Riddles, Juvenile. [1. Puzzles.] I. Titles II. Series:
Kallen, Stuart A., 1955- Giggles, Gags and Groaners.
PN6371.5.K34 1992
818' .5402--dc20   92-14774
                                                                CIP
                                                                AC

International Standard Book Number:	Library of Congress Catalog Card Number:
1-56239-130-5	92-14774

TABLE OF CONTENTS

Puzzle Your Muzzle 5
Check Your Cash 5
Two Trains Traveling 8
Kits, Cats and Sacks 11
Only the Crow Knows......................11
To Tell the Tooth 13
No Fuelin' 14
What's My Line? 14
Who Choose Gum? 16
Oh, Brother 17
Turning the Tide 17
You Say It's Your Birthday 19
The Hole Answer 19
The Hole Answer Part 2 21
Grow to Know.............................21
To Twelve the Truth 23
Skating Away..............................23
I Spy a Trick 24
In the Groove 24
Dog Gone It...............................26
Optical Delusions 26
Ups and Downs 26
Black and White 28
Right on Target 28
Answers 30

PUZZLE YOUR MUZZLE

Life is a puzzle. As baffling as that may seem, it's a mysterious query and a riddle as well. And for most of life's muddling puzzles there are answers. Some are bewildering; some are easy.

But if the answer's too easy then the puzzle's no fun. And fun is no puzzle once the puzzle is done. So begin at the outset, at page number one. And if this makes sense, you've already begun.

CHECK YOUR CASH

Here's a puzzling little puzzle that involves moola, bucks, cash, money. That's a baffling topic to many people. But if you figure this one out you're a financial wizard.

Let's pretend that you're a great guitar player. A billionaire rock star hires you to play guitar on his world tour. You will be playing for millions of people all over the world. The tour will last for one month. The rock star asks you to choose between two methods of payment.

The rock star explains the first method of payment: You may receive one cent on the first day, which doubles every day after that for 31 days. That means that on the second day you would receive 2¢, on the third day you would receive 4¢. On the fourth day you would receive 8¢ and so on.

Then the rock star tells you the other payment method: You would receive $1,000 on the first day and an additional $1,000 every day after that. This way you will receive $2,000 on the second day and $3,000 on the third day. You would receive $4,000 on the fourth day and so on.

Which method of payment would you prefer?

Answer on page 30

TWO TRAINS
TRAVELING

The Zephyr Express leaves Austin, Texas, for Dallas, Texas. The train is traveling through Texas at 70 miles per hour. At the same time, the Lone Star Limited leaves Dallas for Austin. That train is traveling at 90 miles an hour. When they meet, which train is closer to Dallas?

Answer on page 30

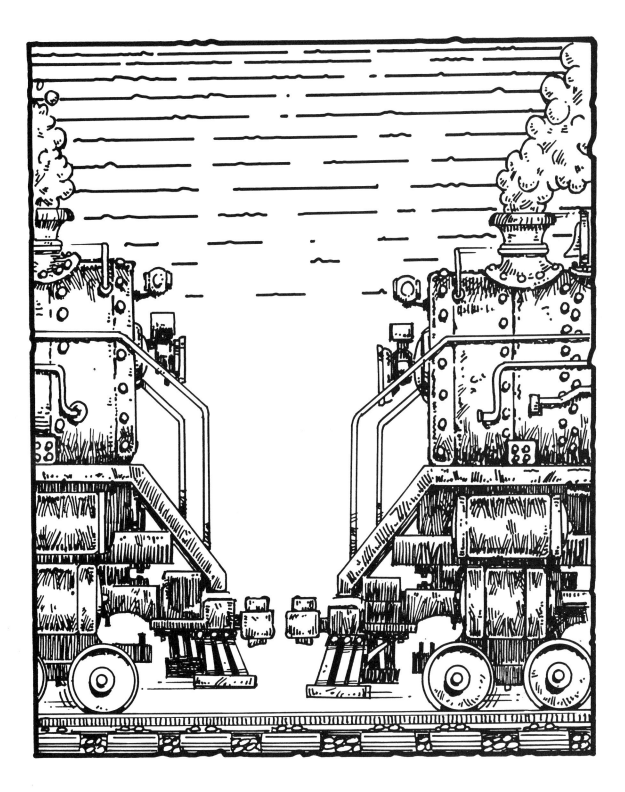

KITS, CATS, AND SACKS

This is an old puzzle.

As I was going to St. Ives, I met a man with 7 wives. Every wife had 7 sacks. Every sack had 7 cats.

Every cat had 7 kits. Kits, cats, sacks, wives; how many were going to St. Ives?

Answer on page 30

ONLY THE CROW KNOWS

A hunter saw 14 crows on a fence. He shot two of them. How many crows remain?

Answer on page 30

TO TELL THE TOOTH

The town of Bigbore is near the North Pole. There are no other towns for hundreds of miles. A woman moves to Bigbore. In the middle of the night she has a horrible tooth ache. The woman needs to visit a dentist. There are two dentists in Bigbore.

Dentist number one has a shiny new office with modern equipment. He has beautiful teeth that show obvious signs of excellent dental work. Dentist number two has a shabby office with old equipment. His teeth are bad and show signs of lousy dental work. Which dentist should the woman choose?

Answer on page 30

NO FUELIN'

A biker is riding down the highway when his motorcycle runs out of gas. He walks to a nearby farm. The biker needs exactly 2 gallons of gas to fill up his motorcycle. The farmer says he can help the biker.

The farmer has a large tank holding 100 gallons of gas. The farmer also has one 5-gallon gas can and one 8-gallon gas can. How can the biker measure exactly 2 gallons for his empty cycle?

Answer on page 31

WHAT'S MY LINE?

The man who owns the movie theater wants to start the movie. First, he must wait until everyone is in the theater. He asks the ticket taker how many kids are still in the ticket line.

The ticket taker replies, "There is 1 kid in front of 2 kids, a kid behind 2 kids, and a kid between 2 kids." How many kids are in the movie line?

Answer on page 31

15

WHO CHOOSE GUM?

Andy and Sandy wanted to buy some gum from a gumball machine. The gum costs one cent apiece. Inside the machine there are 20 purple gumballs and 20 green gumballs. How many pennies would Andy and Sandy have to put into the machine before they could each be certain of sharing a gumball of the same color?

Answer on page 31

OH, BROTHER

The police officer's brother died and left all his money to his only brother. The police officer never received any money although it was legally paid. Why didn't the police officer get any money?

Answer on page 31

TURNING THE TIDE

A ship is anchored in a harbor. It has a rope ladder 8 feet long hanging over the side. The rungs on the ladder are one foot apart with the first rung touching the water. If the tide rises at 4 inches an hour, how long would it be before the ladder is half under water?

Answer on page 31

18

YOU SAY IT'S YOUR BIRTHDAY

Ted is 8 years old. Fred is 4 years old. Ned is 6 years old. What is the total number of birthdays that Ted, Fred, and Ned have had between them?

Answer on page 31

THE HOLE ANSWER

The Iggy and Ziggy want to dig a swimming pool in their backyard. They hire a construction crew to dig them a pool. It takes 2 men 10 days to dig a hole 10 feet deep. How long would it take 1 man to dig half a hole?

Answer on page 32

20

THE HOLE ANSWER PART 2

How much dirt can be removed from a hole 5 feet wide, 3 feet long, and 6 feet deep?

Answer on page 32

GROW TO KNOW

Sally has a tree growing in her backyard. Sally's mom measured Sally's height against the tree when Sally was 5 years old. Sally's mom made a mark at 3 feet to show Sally's height. If the tree grows 2 feet a year, how high would the mark be in 5 years?

Answer on page 32

TO TWELVE THE TRUTH

The man at the coin shop sells sets of newly minted coins. There are 12 one-dollar coins in a dozen. How many twenty-five-cent coins are in a dozen?

Answer on page 32

SKATING AWAY

Sue starts roller skating at 2 o'clock. She wants to skate to a mall on the other side of town. It takes Sue 77 minutes to reach the mall. Ann starts roller skating to the same mall as Sue. She also leaves her house at 2 o'clock. It takes Ann 1 hour and 17 minutes to reach the mall. Who gets to the mall first, Sue or Ann?

Answer on page 32

I SPY A TRICK

A spy's wife said that her husband died of shock while he was asleep. She said that the spy was dreaming that an enemy captured him and was about to shoot him. Meanwhile, a truck was driving down the spy's street when it backfired. The spy heard the noise in his dreams, thought it was a gunshot, and died immediately. What's wrong with this story?

Answer on page 32

IN THE GROOVE

The jazz musician had two phonograph records. One record was 23 minutes long. The other record was 18 minutes long. Which record had the most grooves on it?

Answer on page 32

DOG GONE IT

Which has more tails — one dog or no dogs?

Answer on page 32

OPTICAL DELUSIONS

Lines with arrows on them can be misleading. Which line would you say is longer? Measure them to find out.

UPS AND DOWNS

A line that runs up and down is a *vertical* line. A line that runs side to side is a *horizontal* line.

That is why the place where the ground meets the sky is called the *horizon.* Sometimes these lines can play tricks on our eyes.

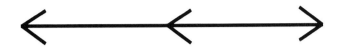

In this illustration, which line is longer, the vertical line or the horizontal line?

Measure them to find out.

BLACK AND WHITE

Black and white boxes can baffle your eyes. Which square is larger, the white square inside the black square or the black square inside the white square? Measure them to find out.

RIGHT ON TARGET

This illusion might make you dizzy. Do you think that the box in the circle is perfectly square? Measure it to find out.

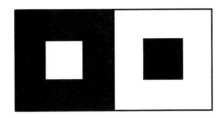

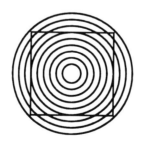

ANSWERS:

Answer to Check Your Cash: *If you were paid $1000 plus $2000 plus $3000, after 31 days you would have almost $541,000. That's a lot of money. But if you were paid 1 penny on the first day, 2 pennies on the second day, 4 pennies on the third day, after 31 days the total would be more than one billion dollars. That's a lot of coin!*

Answer to Two Trains Traveling: *No matter which train was traveling faster, they would both be the same distance from Dallas. That is because they both meet at the same place.*

Answer to Kits, Cats and Sacks: *Only the narrator is going to St. Ives so the answer is one. The first line says, "As I was going to St. Ives, I met a man with seven wives." "I" was the only one going to St. Ives. If "I" met someone along the way they were probably going in the opposite direction.*

Answer to Only the Crow Knows: *Only the two dead crows remain. The rest flew away when the gun went off.*

Answer to Tell the Tooth: *The woman should choose the dentist that has the shabby office and the bad teeth. There are only two dentists in Bigbore. Dentists cannot work on their own teeth. Therefore, the dentist with the bad teeth must have worked on the dentist with the good teeth and visa versa.*

Answer to No Fuelin': *This is how the biker would get 2 gallons of gas in one can. First fill the 5 gallon can and empty it into the 8 gallon can. Then refill the 5 gallon can and pour as much as possible into the 8 gallon can.*

This will be 3 gallons. After the biker pours the three gallons out of the 5 gallon can, 2 gallons of gas will remain. Then he should say "tank you" to the farmer.

Answer to What's My Line?: *There are only three kids in line. The ticket taker had described their position in three different ways.*

Answer to Who Choose Gum: *Andy and Sandy would have to put three pennies in the gumball machine before they could share a gumball of the same color. After the second penny, they would have either 2 gumballs of the same color or 2 gumballs of different colors. A third penny would insure that the gumballs were of both colors.*

Answer to Oh, Brother: *The police officer was a woman. The police officer's brother died and left all his money to his only brother.*

Answer to Turning the Tide: *The ladder will never go under the water. When the tide rises the ship rises with it. The ladder is attached to the ship so it rises too.*

Answer to You Say It's Your Birthday: *Ted, Fred, and Ned have had 3 birthdays. The may have celebrated 18 birthdays between them. But a birthday is only counted as the day a person is born.*

Answer to The Hole Answer: *You can't dig half a hole.*

Answer to The Hole Answer Part 2:   *No dirt can be removed from a hole 5 feet wide, 3 feet long, and 6 feet deep. A hole is a cavity with nothing in it.*

Answer to Grow to Know: *The mark would still be at 3 feet. Trees grow from the top.*

Answer to To Twelve the Truth: *There are 12 twenty-five cent coins in a dozen. A dozen of anything contains 12 items.*

Answer to Skating Away: *Ann and Sue reach the mall at the same time. 77 minutes is the same amount of time as 1 hour and 17 minutes. There are 60 minutes in 1 hour, 60 + 17 = 77.*

Answer to I Spy a Trick: *If the spy died in his sleep, how could his wife know what he was dreaming?*

Answer to In the Groove: *Both records have the same amount of grooves--one. The groove starts at the outside edge of the record and goes around and around and around until it reaches the end.*

Answer to Dog Gone It: *One dog has one tail. But no dog has two tails. Therefore no dog has more tails than one dog. Dog gone it!*